CW01629061

Julian Hunt has defended HMO cases across the country. He has dealt with issues concerning licensing, management regulation breaches, whether HMOs are compliant with fire safety legislation and local council policies. He has worked with managing agents, landlords and professional investors along with planning consultants. He is a barrister of thirteen years' call and was a Senior Crown Prosecutor in his early years. He has a website at:

https://housing-act-prosecution-defence-barrister.co.uk/

Julian was educated at Cambridge University and is a Lincoln's Inn Lord Denning award winner. He lives in London.

A Practical Guide to the Law of Houses in Multiple Occupation

A Practical Guide to the Law of Houses in Multiple Occupation

Julian Hunt MA (Cantab),
Barrister (Lincoln's Inn)

Law Brief Publishing

Published 2018 by Law Brief Publishing, an imprint of Law Brief Publishing Ltd
30 The Parks
Minehead
Somerset
TA24 8BT

www.lawbriefpublishing.com

Paperback: 978-1-911035-65-7

To Tammy, Teddy, Dad and Brenda

PREFACE

HMO legislation used to be made up of a hodge-podge of laws. In 2004 the Government in response to growing concerns over HMOs decided to regulate the industry to improve standards for tenants. Many were and are some of the most vulnerable individuals in society.

As Lord Justice Lewison said in *Nottingham City Council v Parr* [2017] EWCA Civ 188:

> *"Until the passing of the Housing Act 2004 local housing authorities had a patchwork of powers to deal with unsatisfactory conditions in HMOs. These were in essence reactive powers dependent on a complaint by an occupier. The introduction of a compulsory licensing scheme, which had been advocated by housing charities and others for many years, established a more proactive regime. HMOs are typically occupied by those who cannot afford better accommodation, such as students, people on low incomes or foreign nationals. These classes of persons are or may be vulnerable, and the imposition of standards on HMOs is intended to protect their housing conditions and hence their health and welfare"*

Since 2004 there has been a large increase in the amount of litigation undertaken by Local Authority Environmental Health Teams (also called Rogue Landlord Units or HMO Enforcement Teams depending on the Local Authority) in relation to regulating and licencing HMO. This book focuses on the law from a practical perspective in relation to defending Local Authority prosecutions or litigation in this area. It focuses on breaches of the Housing Act 2004 in relation to HMOs.

It deals with some of the most common issues practitioners will find in handling such cases from the criminal and regulatory perspective. Due to the nature of HMO law it straddles both the world of property law and criminal law. What is an HMO? What are the common core issues HMO owners and agents face in legal proceedings? How are HMO cases sentenced? I also hope that this book will be of counsel and guidance to managing agents and landlord who are, of course, the individuals facing a world of unlimited fines and publication on name and shame council websites. It should be on their reading list. I finally hope it will be of some use to those defending (or preparing a prosecution) for an unlicenced HMO or an HMO that has breached a management regulation.

I finish with two pleas. There appears to be little consistency in which HMO owners and managing agents are prosecuted across the country. Some Housing Officers prosecute cases other officers would not touch. More consistency would be a good thing as would more education for managing agents and landlords on the harsh HMO regime they face and that with the rewards of higher returns come the higher risks of prosecution.

The Law is current as of 13th May 2018.

Julian Hunt
London
May 2018

CONTENTS

CHAPTER ONE
WHAT IS A HOUSE IN MULTIPLE OCCUPATION (HMO)?

One of the most important aspects of HMO law is defining what and what is not an HMO. In addition to defining an HMO one then needs to consider whether the HMO (all of which come under the ambit of the Management Regulations) is one which is required to be licenced or not. Hence as well as working out if your property is an HMO you also need to consider whether the property requires a licence (either under what is called additional licensing schemes or under the mandatory scheme). If a prosecution occurs it is fundamental to the prosecution case that the Local Authority make the Court sure beyond reasonable doubt that the property in question is or was an HMO at the time of the offence. If it wasn't or isn't then all offending falls away. There are further a number of exemptions to the HMO rules as to properties which, although ostensibly are HMOs, are in fact exempt from HMO rules. There are also provisions as to which type of persons are deemed or presumed to live in the HMO as their sole or main residence.

Important questions to be asked

Before I go on to the legislation, the important practical questions to ask are:

a) How many people unrelated are in residence in the property as their main property?

b) What is the evidence of them being in residence as their main property?

c) Does the property come within the ambit of the definitions in the Housing Act 2004?

d) Is the property once which requires either a mandatory licence or is it within an area which is subject to additional licensing?

e) Is it within an area subject to selective licensing?

f) Does an exemption apply as to whether it is an HMO?

The five tests

Under section 254(1)(a)-(e) there are five tests as to whether a property is an HMO. Some are more common than others. These are:

a) The standard test;

b) The self-contained test;

c) The converted building test;

d) A property declared to be an HMO under section 255;

e) A HMO defined under Section 257.

A declaration that a property is an HMO under section 255 is rare. The more common HMO permutations are a-c.

Standard Test

Under Section 254(2) a building or part of a building meets the standard test for an HMO if:

> *"(a) it consists of one or more units of living accommodation not consisting of a self-contained flat or flats;*
>
> *(b) the living accommodation is occupied by persons who do not form a single household (see section 258);*
>
> *(c) the living accommodation is occupied by those persons as their only or main residence or they are to be treated as so occupying it (see section 259);*
>
> *(d) their occupation of the living accommodation constitutes the only use of that accommodation;*
>
> *(e) rents are payable or other consideration is to be provided in respect of at least one of those persons' occupation of the living accommodation; and*
>
> *(f) two or more of the households who occupy the living accommodation share one or more basic amenities or the living accommodation is lacking in one or more basic amenities."*

This definition will cover most standard shared flats. Unless deemed to be occupying it as their main residence the property must be their only or main residence. Students, in particular, come under the deeming provisions (and are to be treated as so occupying it) under section 259 if the property is their residence for the purposes of a full-time course in further or higher education.

What is Sole Residence?

Others to be treated as occupying the property as their sole or main residence include those

a) in a refuge managed by a voluntary organization due to domestic violence from their partner (section 259(2)(b) and (3));

b) a migrant worker or a seasonal worker whose occupation of the building or part is made partly in consideration of his employment within the United Kingdom, whether or not other charges are payable in respect of that occupation and where the building or part is provided by, or on behalf of, his employer or an agent or employee of his employer;

c) an asylum seeker or a dependent of an asylum seeker who has been provided with accommodation under section 95 of the Immigration and Asylum Act 1999 and which is funded partly or wholly by the National Asylum Support Service

The phrase "sole or main residence" in the Court of Appeal authority of *Williams v Horsham* [2004] 1 WLR 1137 was held to mean the following by Lord Philips MR:

> *"All this reinforces the conclusion (which is one that we would have reached without reference to the dictionary) that in section 6(5) of the Act "sole or main residence" refers to premises in which the taxpayer actually resides. The qualification "sole or main" addresses the fact that a person may reside in more than one place. We think that it is probably impossible to produce a definition of "main residence" that will provide the appropriate*

test in all circumstances. Usually, however, a person's main residence will be the dwelling that a reasonable onlooker, with knowledge of the material facts, would regard as that person's home at the material time. That test may not always be an easy one to apply, but we have no doubt as to the conclusion to which it leads in the present case."

Although for a council tax sole residency case this leading authority can be transposed for HMO cases. (See also *R (On the Application of Bennett) v Copeland DC* [2004] EWCA Civ 672 where the reasoning in *Williams* was affirmed).

Self-Contained Test

The self-contained test is defined in section 254(3) as

"(3) A part of a building meets the self-contained flat test if—

(a) it consists of a self-contained flat; and

(b) paragraphs (b) to (f) of subsection (2) apply (reading references to the living accommodation concerned as references to the flat)"

In other words, it is the same as the standard test but with the phrase "living accommodation" substituted for "flat". Self-contained flats are defined as a separate set of premises (whether or not on the same floor)—

a) which forms part of a building;

b) either the whole or a material part of which lies above or below some other part of the building; and

c) in which all three basic amenities are available for the exclusive use of its occupants

Converted Building Test

Under the converted building test a building or part of a building is part of an HMO if:

"(a) it is a converted building;

(b) it contains one or more units of living accommodation that do not consist of a self-contained flat or flats (whether or not it also contains any such flat or flats);

(c) the living accommodation is occupied by persons who do not form a single household (see section 258);

(d) the living accommodation is occupied by those persons as their only or main residence or they are to be treated as so occupying it (see section 259);

(e) their occupation of the living accommodation constitutes the only use of that accommodation; and

(f) rents are payable or other consideration is to be provided in respect of at least one of those persons' occupation of the living accommodation."

The test is again virtually identical to the other tests but with the proviso of being a converted building. A converted building is defined as a building or part of a building consisting of living accommodation in which one or more units of such accommodation have been created since the building or part was constructed.

Note the use of the past tense – it must have been converted since the building was constructed.

Section 257 HMO

This section applies to self-contained flats in blocks which were built not in compliance with at their minimum building standards as of 1st June 1992. In other words, self-contained flats not built in conformity with the 1991 Building Regulations that came into force on 1st June 1992 (and still do not comply with them) are regulated as HMOs. In addition, less than two-thirds of the flats must be owner-occupied. Note that it is for the LA to prove that any block of flats comes within this exemption in any prosecution under the section 257 route. The practical issue here is finding the relevant building control certificates or conveyancing documents to show that the converted flats were not in conformity with the 1991 Building Regulations if no works have been undertaken to bring them to them up to the necessary building standards. It is critical to ask the LA what the proof is that the property is a section 257 HMO – why do they say it does not comply with pre-1992 building standards? Where are their records to prove this? Here is the relevant legislation:

> *"(1) For the purposes of this section a* "converted block of flats" *means a building or part of a building which–*
>
> *(a) has been converted into, and*
>
> *(b) consists of,*
>
> *self-contained flats.*
>
> *(2) This section applies to a converted block of flats if–*

(a) building work undertaken in connection with the conversion did not comply with the appropriate building standards and still does not comply with them; and

(b) less than two-thirds of the self-contained flats are owner-occupied.

(3) In subsection (2) "appropriate building standards" *means–*

(a) in the case of a converted block of flats–

(i) on which building work was completed before 1st June 1992 or which is dealt with by regulation 20 of the Building Regulations 1991 (S.I. 1991/2768), and

(ii) which would not have been exempt under those Regulations,

building standards equivalent to those imposed, in relation to a building or part of a building to which those Regulations applied, by those Regulations as they had effect on 1st June 1992; and

(b) in the case of any other converted block of flats, the requirements imposed at the time in relation to it by regulations under section 1 of the Building Act 1984 (c. 55).

(4) For the purposes of subsection (2) a flat is "owner-occupied" if it is occupied–

(a) by a person who has a lease of the flat which has been granted for a term of more than 21 years,

(b) by a person who has the freehold estate in the converted block of flats, or

(c) by a member of the household of a person within paragraph (a) or (b).

(5) The fact that this section applies to a converted block of flats (with the result that it is a house in multiple occupation under section 254(1)(e)), does not affect the status of any flat in the block as a house in multiple occupation.

(6) In this section "self-contained flat" *has the same meaning as in section 254."*

Section 255 Declaration

There is limited power in section 255 for LAs to declare certain buildings under the standard, self-contained or converted building test to be an HMO with an appeal by way of a re-hearing at the Property Tribunal if the LA believes that to a significant extent the property is being used as an HMO. Using this difficultly worded section certain examples of significant but not sole use might include a hotel catering for short term guests or a hostel accommodating permanent residents.

Meaning of a single household

Section 258 sets out the people who are to be regarded as forming single households. This broad definition includes:

a) Members of the same family as a husband and wife or a couple living together as husband and wife (or in the equivalent same sex relationship);

b) Relatives defined as including parents, grandparents, children, grandchildren, brothers, sisters, uncles, aunts, nephews or cousins, or stepchildren.

c) One person being a relative of one member of a couple and the other a relative of the other member of the couple.

In short, relationships by blood or marriage will mean that the individuals concerned do count as a single household. Others to be regarded as forming a single household (with a family) under Regulation 3 of the Licensing and Management of Houses in Multiple Occupation and Other Houses (Miscellaneous Provisions) (England) Regulations 2006 include workers for a family living in accommodation provided as consideration for the work they perform (which must be of an exclusively domestic nature) for the person they share with and where <u>they do not pay rent or any other consideration</u> for the living accommodation.

Work usually carried out by an au pair, nanny, carer, servant, maid, cleaner, gardener, chauffeur, cook, cleaner, butler, secretary or personal assistant is to be regarded as work of a "domestic nature". What is important to ensure that any domestic staff come within the exclusionary ambit if they share accommodation is to ensure they do not pay extra rent for their room or lodging.

Others to be regarded as forming a single household are adult placement carers under the Approved Placement Schemes (England) Regulations 2004 so long as that carer provides care in the living accommodation for not more than three service users along with those placed with foster carers. The key to this section is that unrelated individuals will almost invariably be caught out by the provisions unless within this very tightly delineated group

One point to note is the situation of a family moving in and telling the managing agent or owner they are all related when in fact they are not by blood. Here there is a question of whether the letting agent or owner has a reasonable excuse in believing them and thus not complying with the Management Regulations or having the property licenced as the case may be.

In *Paramaguru v London Borough of Ealing* [2018] EWHC 373 (Admin) a child under 18 and indeed a new born baby were held to be "residents" in the case of property, under planning law, used as a Class C4 HMO (for use of not more than six residents as an HMO). That property had compromised six adults and four children and hence the owner had breached a planning enforcement notice. The purpose of all HMO legislation is to protect the most vulnerable from danger and an approach deeming the children not to be treated as residents would run counter to the purpose of HMO law. (See para 37 of *Paramaguru* where the comments of Buxton LJ on the special need to guard against the risks of danger in HMO's in *Brent London Borough Council v Reynolds* 2002 HLR 15 are cited).

CHAPTER TWO
EXEMPTED HMOs

A number of properties are exempted from the HMO regime. Under Schedule 14 of the Housing Act 2004 the key exemptions are:

a) *Any building which is occupied only by two persons who form two households.* Three or more unrelated people are required for the Management Regulations to bite and any additional licencing schemes.

b) <u>Owner occupied buildings with two or fewer tenants are exempt</u>. The wording of this important exemption in Schedule 14 paragraph 6 reads:

> *"(1) Any building which is occupied only by persons within the following paragraphs–*
>
> *(a) one or more persons who have, whether in the whole or any part of it, either the freehold estate or a leasehold interest granted for a term of more than 21 years;*
>
> *(b) any member of the household of such a person or persons;*
>
> *(c) no more than such number of other persons as is specified for the purposes of this paragraph in regulations made by the appropriate national authority. <u>(The number is two at present)"</u>*

The upshot of paragraph 6 is that a live-in landlord who has three people living in their home as occupiers must abide by the same regulations as the landlord with seven or eight individuals in a large, rambling properties (but without the need for mandatory licencing).

c) Buildings controlled or managed by public sector bodies including local housing authorities and registered providers of social housing

d) Social housing managed or controlled by a profit-making registered provider of social housing

e) Buildings controlled or managed by a co-operative society

f) Buildings occupied solely or principally by students for the purpose of a full time further or high education course at a specified educational establishment and where the person managing or controlling it is that educational establishment. The current list of specified educational institutions for England (covering most universities) is listed in the Houses in Multiple Occupation (Specified Educational Establishments) (England) Regulations 2016.

g) Buildings principally occupied by religious communities whose principal occupation is prayer, education, contemplation or the relief of suffering.

The two most important exemptions are the owner occupier exemption and where a property has two or fewer households occupying it. If the LA contend that the flat has a third person in it (not on the tenancy agreement to give an example) it is well worth enquiring whether the landlord or agent gave permission for this third person to occupy the flat and whether it is their sole or main residence.

CHAPTER THREE
MANDATORY LICENCING

At present non-section 257 HMOs that are three storeys or more and have five or more people living in two or more separate households are required to have a mandatory license under the Licensing of Houses in Multiple Occupation (Prescribed Descriptions) (England) Order 2006. This is an important provision as it has always meant that large HMOs as well as coming under the Management Regulations have required licensing involving payments of fees to Local Authorities and the filling in of lengthy forms.

In addition, this has meant that the property is put on the LA's HMO register as a licenced HMO. LA Housing Officers will further go around to inspect the property before a licence is issued for the property. License conditions are issued with the risk of a prosecution if not abided by. Many prosecutions are for owners not licensing an HMO that comes within the mandatory licensing criteria (or indeed the additional licensing criteria) or for breaches of licencing conditions.

These large HMOs are seen as high risk and LA's focus their energies on these properties. The consultation document "Licensing in the Private Rented Sector" published by the Office of the Deputy Prime Minister in 2004 made it clear why the policy target would be these HMOs:

> *"We intend to use secondary legislation to apply mandatory licensing to HMOs with 3 or more storeys and 5 or more residents who constitute more than one household (other than where the building comprises self contained blocks or certain exempted categories). We are targeting these properties because:*
>
> *Physical conditions in some of these HMOs are very poor.*

There is a significantly increased risk of dying or being injured in a fire in such properties. The fatality rate in HMOs of three or more storeys is around four times higher than that for one or two storey HMOs

A range of health, safety and general welfare problems for residents can arise where structural conditions are unsuitable for the number of persons accommodated, or where conversion has been poorly undertaken.

There are often problems of management in such HMOs, especially where facilities are shared.

Tenants in these HMOs are often vulnerable and may not have access to other housing options."

Storeys and their meaning

The current 2006 Order defines the term "storey" as follows under article 3:

"3) The following storeys shall be taken into account when calculating whether the HMO or any part of it comprises three storeys or more—]=

(a) any basement if—

(i) it is used wholly or partly as living accommodation;

(ii) it has been constructed, converted or adapted for use wholly or partly as living accommodation;

(iii) it is being used in connection with, and as an integral part of, the HMO; or

(iv) it is the only or principal entry into the HMO from the street.

(b) any attic if—

(i) it is used wholly or partly as living accommodation;

(ii) it has been constructed, converted or adapted for use wholly or partly as living accommodation, or

(iii) it is being used in connection with, and as an integral part of, the HMO;

(c) where the living accommodation is situated in a part of a building above business premises, each storey comprising the business premises;

(d) where the living accommodation is situated in a part of a building below business premises, each storey comprising the business premises;

(e) any mezzanine floor not used solely as a means of access between two adjoining floors if—

(i) it is used wholly or mainly as living accommodation; or

(ii) it is being used in connection with, and as an integral part of, the HMO; and

(f) any other storey that is used wholly or partly as living accommodation or in connection with, and as an integral part of, the HMO."

What is a storey?

There has been some litigation on the meaning of a storey and whether a self-contained flat in a tower block (with say five people or more) is a licensable HMO. In *Unite v Islington* [2013] EWHC 508 (Admin) it was held that it is the HMO that must comprise the three storeys and not the building in which the HMO is to be found. Article 3(3)(f) of the 2006 Order did not in that case bring the cluster flats in Charles Morton Court into the licensing regime. Each flat was on one story and self-contained. After including the ground-floor, business premises in the calculation, the three-storey threshold was not reached. Blake J, in that case, stated:

> *"29 In my judgment, Mr Arden's submissions are to be preferred to those of Mr Drabble. The need for 'clarity' stressed in the consultation may seem ironic given the legitimate division of opinion as to the meaning of the Order reflected in the LACORS document, but it was the search for a comprehensive approach as identified in the consultation that lead to the drafting of Article 3(3) as a supplement to the general principle of Article 3(2).*
>
> *30 Article 3(3) does not substitute for Article 3(2) and deprive it of its natural meaning, but sets out special rules for the limited purpose of bringing business premises and certain uses associated with the HMO into the equation whereas they would otherwise be excluded.*
>
> ***31 It is the HMO that must comprise the three storeys and not the building in which an HMO happens to be found.***
>
> ***32 The hapless tenant of a "purpose built" flat in a tower block who sub-lets a flat to two households of five people, should not be at risk of prosecution for failing to obtain a licence, as the Order was not intended to apply in such circumstances. If there is a perceived local need to regulate activity, the local authority can promulgate its own supplementary scheme"***

In *Bristol City Council v Digs (Bristol) Ltd* [2014] EWHC 869 (Admin) it was held that the word "storey" in the Licensing of Houses in Multiple Occupation (Prescribed Descriptions) (England) Order 2006 article 3 should ordinarily be understood as meaning the whole floor, namely the space on a given level within a building. Stairs between floors could not, in themselves, be "storeys" unless they were within article 3(3)(f) because they were used as living accommodation, or were used as an integral part of the house in multiple occupation.

Burnett J held in relation to whether the meaning of a story in the context of living accommodation:

> ***30 The question whether any storey is used wholly or partly as living accommodation is also a question of fact.*** *"Living accommodation" is not defined in the 2006 Order or in the 2004 Act. There is a clue in article 3(3)(c) that it does not include lobbies and landings leading to a self-contained flat because the reference is to "living accommodation ... above business premises" which necessarily must be served by a means of access. The District Judge recorded that one of the admissions on which the case proceeded before him was that the students had, on the day on which the facts were determined, left some of their belongings in the private hallway. There was some suggestion that such action leant weight to an argument that it was being used partly as living accommodation. Mr Bhose, rightly in my view, did not press that argument. He suggested that the fact that these spaces were demised to the occupiers of the upper maisonette was sufficient to engage the licensing provisions, irrespective of what was actually done with them.*
>
> ***31 There may well be circumstances where a landing or hallway is used wholly or partly as living accommodation. The space may be sufficient for use as a small room for all sorts of purposes, and it may be used as such. For example,***

> ***by placing a sofa and a television there, a desk with computer and chair (perhaps more likely with students) or even a baby's cot. But the exiguous and transitory nature of leaving a few belongings in a hallway at the bottom of two flights of stairs does not, in my judgment, turn the space into living accommodation.***

Change from October 2018

It is vital to note that from 1st October 2018 to have more HMOs come under the mandatory licensing regime, the Licensing of Houses in Multiple Occupation (Prescribed Description) (England) Order 2018 will revoke the 2006 order with the simple fact that the requirement for a property to have three stories or more before coming under the mandatory regime will not be required.

This will require many more HMOs to be licenced under the mandatory regime as they will merely need to be occupied by five or more people living in two or more separate households with a review of this new onerous provision by April 2023.

Licensing Offences

Controlling or managing a property without a license under section 72(1) of the Housing Act 2004 without a reasonable excuse is punishable by an unlimited fine. There are no recent reported cases of the ambit of reasonable excuse in the context of licensing offences under the modern section 72 or Management Regulations. In *London Borough of Wandsworth v Sparling* (1988) 20 H.L.R. 169 in relation to the old HMO management regulations – framed in similar language – it was held that the Local Authority, in keeping rents which could have been used for the upkeep of a property by an impecunious owner, were the authors of their own misfortune. The Court, giving some general guidance, held:

> *"In relation to that separate offence of failing to comply without reasonable excuse, the question of what is or is not in any particular case reasonable excuse is in my judgment entirely a matter for the justices, subject always to the subject matter in question being as a matter of law capable of constituting reasonable excuse. I must say for my part in the present case, having regard to the council's receipt of the rent and council's holding of the capital fund, the Justices would be well capable of finding that there was here reasonable excuse had the second offence been properly charged. As I have indicated, it was not."*

In this case the conduct and behaviour of the LA was criticised. This is plainly a country mile from the pure ignorance of a landlord or the shutting of eyes to very obvious breaches of Management Regulations and licencing obligations.

Other offences under section 72 include being in control of a licenced HMO and <u>knowingly</u> permitting another person to occupy the house resulting in the house being occupied by more households or persons than is authorized by the license without a reasonable excuse or breaches of licencing conditions without a reasonable excuse.

It is worth at this stage noting *Nottingham City Council v Parr* [2017] EWCA Civ 188 with leave granted to the Supreme Court in which the Court of Appeal held that a condition as to the <u>personal characteristic</u> of the occupant in the licence conditions – that they had to be a student – was lawful. The full wording of the condition held to be lawful as substituted by the First Tier Tribunal had read: "*The second floor front bedroom may only be used for sleeping accommodation by a person engaged in full-time education and who resides in the dwelling for a maximum period of 10 calendar months over a period of one year."* In short, the Court held that conditions can regulate *who,* via general characteristics, lives in a property as well as *how* they live in the property. Lord Justice Lewison held:

> *"There is no doubt, in my judgment, that the general characteristics of occupiers are relevant in some contexts connected both with HMOs and with housing standards generally. Thus one of the standard conditions which must be imposed in a licence is a requirement that the manager of the HMO must demand references from persons who wish to occupy the house: Sched. 4 para 2. Necessarily a reference is likely to comment on the personal characteristics of an occupier.* ***In some cases it will be relevant to investigate not only the personal characteristics of occupiers, but also what they do. For example in deciding whether a house is occupied by a single household or more than one household, persons carrying out domestic services are regarded as occupying the same household as their employer if they are occupying rent free tied accommodation in the same building: The Licensing and Management of Houses in Multiple Occupation and Other Houses (Miscellaneous Provisions) (England) Regulations 2006 reg. 3.*** *It must, therefore, be relevant in some cases to investigate whether someone is actually carrying out domestic services. Likewise, a full-time student is regarded as occupying accommodation as his only or main residence if it is occupied for the purpose of his full time course. So it must in some cases be relevant to investigate what kind of course a student is pursuing. Some religious communities are outside the HMO scheme, but only if their "principal occupation" is prayer, contemplation, education or the relief of suffering: Housing Act 2004 Sched. 14 para. 5. It may therefore be relevant to investigate what is the principal occupation of a religious community."*

CHAPTER FOUR THE MEANING OF BEING IN CONTROL OR MANAGING AN HMO

Allegations in relation to HMO's will make reference in their wording to the person <u>in control or managing</u> the property as being the liable party. Section 263 of the Housing Act 2004 sets out the general and widely framed definition of a person in control of managing.

It provides:

"(1) In this Act "person having control", in relation to premises, means (unless the context otherwise requires) the person who receives the rack-rent of the premises (whether on his own account or as agent or trustee of another person), or who would so receive it if the premises were let at a rack-rent.

(2) In subsection (1) "rack-rent" means a rent which is not less than two-thirds of the full net annual value of the premises.

(3) In this Act "person managing" means, in relation to premises, the person who, being an owner or lessee of the premises—

(a) receives (whether directly or through an agent or trustee) rents or other payments from—

(i) in the case of a house in multiple occupation, persons who are in occupation as tenants or licensees of parts of the premises; and

(ii) in the case of a house to which Part 3 applies (see section 79(2)), persons who are in occupation as tenants or licensees of parts of the premises, or of the whole of the premises; or

(b) would so receive those rents or other payments but for having entered into an arrangement (whether in pursuance of a court order or otherwise) with another person who is not an owner or lessee of the premises by virtue of which that other person receives the rents or other payments;

and includes, where those rents or other payments are received through another person as agent or trustee, that other person.

(4) In its application to Part 1, subsection (3) has effect with the omission of paragraph (a)(ii).

(5) References in this Act to any person involved in the management of a house in multiple occupation or a house to which Part 3 applies (see section 79(2)) include references to the person managing it."

In relation to a section 257 HMO section 61 (7) provides:

"In this Part the "person having control" in respect of a section 257 HMO is –

'(a) in relation to an HMO in respect of which no person has been granted a long lease of a flat within the HMO, the person who receives the rack rent for the HMO whether on his own account or as an agent or trustee of another person..."'

The definition hence ensnares the majority of HMO landlords and agents receiving a fee from property. <u>The core point is that the definition is, in blunt terms, based on receipt of money – who</u>

gets the money or, as a trustee or agent, a percentage of the income from the property. If prosecuting such cases it is vital to establish evidence showing that the accused individual is the person in control or managing the property in question. This can be as simple as bank statements exhibited showing funds being transferred to an agent or landlord as the case may be from the tenants. Whatever the contractual relationship between agent and landlord via any management agreement liability itself is established on the basis of the statutory foundation in section 263.

Who is responsible for the rack-rent?

In *Urban Lettings v London Borough of Haringay* [2015] UKUT 104 (LC) the court noted the difference between section 61(7) and section 263(1) – namely the omission of liability of the person who would receive rack rent if the property was let at rack rent.

Reviewing the authorities on who should be liable as the person in control for an HMO when ostensible no-one was receiving the rack rent the Upper Tribunal held:

> *"Whilst it is true that there are no authorities on s 61(7) itself the authorities on the equivalent of ss 263(1) and (2) of the 2004 Act are of considerable assistance. They show to my mind a consistent theme of the Courts seeking to establish and give effect to the policy of the legislation and to avoid a situation where no-one is responsible for the relevant obligations. To my mind these themes emerge clearly from the passages I have set out above."*

Trying to find a solution which avoided no-one being the person in control of an HMO (and this avoided a Rent Repayment Order in Urban Lettings) the Upper Tribunal held:

> *"The owner of an interest in premises who receives the rack rent, as the measure of the value of the premises to an occupier, is a person who ought in justice to be responsible for the discharge of the licensing obligations of the HMO."*

This fits in with Lord Bridges analysis in *Pollway Nominees v London Borough Croydon LBC* [1987] AC 79 (referred to in *Urban Lettings*) who stated:

> *"In all these cases the rationale of the use of the formula to designate the person on whom the relevant obligation is cast is surely plain.* ***The owner of that interest in premises which carries with it the right, actual or potential, to receive the rack rent****, as the measure of the value of the premises to an occupier, is the person who ought in justice to be responsible for the discharge of the liabilities to which the premises by reason of their situation or condition give rise."*

The Upper Tribunal wanted to avoid at all costs the situation of no-one being in control of twelve units of accommodation in this particular case due to the structure of the leases and the arrangements in this case – someone "ought in justice" to be liable as the receiver of rack-rents:

> *"If Mr Maddan's submissions are correct no one would fall within the definition of a person in control with the result that no-one would be liable for the licensing obligations of these three HMOs. The lease from Mrs Hussain to CPR is at less than a rack rent and thus she is not within the definition. The 12*

> *leases from CPR to ULL do not include the common parts merely rights of access over them. It follows (if Mr Maddan is correct) that they are not leases of the HMOs. Equally the 12 leases from ULL to the individual occupiers do not include the common parts and are thus (if Mr Maddan is correct) not leases of the HMOs. As Lord Goff pointed out this would be a very undesirable situation and not one which can have been intended by the legislature."*

Using the words of Lord Bridges the "rights, actual or potential" to receive the rack rent was the appellant company in this case. They were in justice responsible leasing out flats to individual occupiers for the discharge of the licensing obligations in this case.

CHAPTER FIVE THE MANAGEMENT REGULATIONS

In this chapter I go through the HMO Management Regulations (The Management of Houses in Multiple Occupation (England) Regulations 2006) and some of the key issues to look out for when one is summonsed to Court for management breaches in respect of HMO cases. This initial part is not concerned with HMO conversions (i.e. self-contained flats in converted blocks) but with the regulations governing all other HMOs.

Preliminary Points

It is important to note the following:

a) A breach of the regulations means an unlimited fine since March 2015 (up to £5000 before this date). Although fines are often linked to the profit an HMO owner has made they are also linked to the danger that the breach may have caused. Hence, fire breaches are far more serious than mere decorative breaches. The Courts must, of course, take into the means of the company or person managing the HMO but with no guidelines for HMO breaches fines vary from court to court. An offender can ask for a conditional or absolute discharge (especially if there has been no actual danger to the public) but these are very rare. Coupled with payment of the costs to the Local Authority such a punishment might seem fair on very rare occasions but invariably the courts will want to fine landlords and managing agents for these breaches.

b) The Management Regulations afford the person in control, whether it is the managing agent or landlord, a reasonable excuse defence. Many summonses will not mention the reasonable excuse defence but simply lay out the facts of the summons within them.

c) Despite Local Authorities summonsing many HMO owners for these offences there are no reported cases in the higher courts on the interpretation of the actual Management Regulations or indeed of the term "reasonable excuse" within the specific context of the current Management Regulations.

d) Both companies and directors can be summonsed for breaching Management Regulations. Directors are liable if through their consent, connivance or neglect the Management Regulations have been breached.

Personal Liability of Directors

I set out the relevant part of section 251 of the Housing Act as in practice it is of some importance with directors naturally very concerned when personally summonsed to Court and facing criminal liability (which can also be used for licencing offences under the Act)

"Offences by bodies corporate

(1) Where an offence under this Act committed by a body corporate is proved to have been committed with the consent or connivance of, or to be attributable to any neglect on the part of —

(a) a director, manager, secretary or other similar officer of the body corporate, or

(b) a person purporting to act in such a capacity,

he as well as the body corporate commits the offence and is liable to be proceeded against and punished accordingly."

Definitions for personal liability

In *R v Chargot Limited* [2008] UKHL 73 Lord Hope gave useful observations in defining term "neglect" for analogous health and safety prosecutions which can be applied in deciding if the individual director is liable for Management Regulation breaches

In relation to remoteness, it was held:

"it will be a relatively short step for the inference to be drawn that there was connivance or neglect on his part if the circumstances under which the risk arose were under the direction or control of the officer. The more remote his area of responsibility is from those circumstances, the harder it will be to draw that inference."

If the person being prosecuted along with the company is, for instance, the sole director of a small letting agency or the sole director of a company that the tenants pay rent to one should further note these comments of Lord Hope:

"Here too the circumstances will vary from case to case. So no fixed rule can be laid down as to what the prosecution must identify and prove in order to establish that the officer's state of mind was such as to amount to consent, connivance or neglect.

> *In some cases, as where the officer's place of activity was remote from the work place or what was done there was not under his immediate direction and control, this may require the leading of quite detailed evidence of which fair notice may have to be given. In others, where the officer was in day to day contact with what was done there, very little more may be needed."*

In reality, there will often be nothing more than a cigarette paper thin line between the sole director of a company which manages, say, two properties and the company itself. He will not be remote from the work of the company and indeed may be the person dealing and managing the property itself. Even if he delegates some dealing in the property to someone else it may well be that if he maintains oversight of the property (i.e by engaging agents for taking rent only but undertaking all management himself) it is clear that breaches are more likely to be said to emanate due to his neglect or consent. Lord Hope emphasises "day to day" contact as showing how little more would need to be proved to find the director personally liable. If in an HMO case the director does have daily contact (ie administering the property, liaising with tenants and handymen) it is very likely he will by neglect (if the facts of the breach are made out) be liable along with the company.

Tenant duties under the Management Regulations

Although never charged in reality, occupiers also have their own set of mandatory duties under Management Regulations which if breached can result in a fine. One of the difficulties is that if one argues that the occupiers have for instance vandalised fire alarms and hence breached the management regulations which apply to them as well the LA may well argue that as a person in control or manager you ought to have systems in place (including inspections at a regular interval which can be an HMO licence condition) to ensure that such breaches do not occur.

That said, it can be worth reminding Local Authorities, in letters of representation, that tenants or occupiers also have strict legal duties which they may have ridden a coach and horses through leaving the landlord or managing agent the liable party.

Specific duties of tenants

These duties under Regulation 10 of the Management Regulations are:

a) Conducting oneself in a way that will not hinder or frustrate the HMO manager in the performance of his duties;

b) Allowing the manger to enter living accommodation at reasonable times to carry out duties imposed by the Regulations and providing him with any information he may need to carry out his duties;

c) Taking reasonable care to avoid causing damage to anything the manager is under a duty to supply, maintain or repair. This includes fire equipment and other safety measures which are obligatory in HMOs;

d) Storing and disposing of litter in accordance with the HMO manager's arrangements;

e) Complying with the reasonable instructions of the manager in respect of means of escape from fire, prevention of fire and use of fire equipment.

Indeed, in letters of representations to the Local Authority it is worth citing examples of breaches of regulation ten when arguing that the manager has a reasonable excuse. If a tenant, for instance, has broken a smoke alarm or put a plastic bag over it unbeknown to anyone as it has not been picked up on a regular inspection (perhaps due to the tenant locking his room) then it worth citing the occupier's own breaches of the Management Regulation in whether there is a) a public interest in prosecuting and b) whether the landlord is afforded a reasonable excuse defence by these tenant breaches of regulation ten.

Lack of information as to enforcement of Regulation 10

I recently wrote to Her Majesty's Courts and Tribunal Services and asked how many tenants had been prosecuted for offences under regulation ten. HMCTS doesn't keep data on this statistic. I imagine the answer is very few, if any, with the enforcement policy of most Local Authorities to ignore breaches of the Management Regulations by tenants (however egregious) and simply focus on landlords.

Drafting of summonses

I will go through the key regulations and what to bear in mind when dealing with these cases. It should be noted that the drafting of the summonses varies from authority to authority. Some prosecuting authorities will draft very detailed summonses setting out with clarity the exact breach alleged. This is particularly important for the more general regulatory breaches such as not keeping properties in good decorative repair or breaches such as a garden or other outdoors area being unsafe or untidy. Other prosecuting authorities will simply pay lip-service to the elements of the offence with a very general allegation. The problem here is that one then has to cross-reference the breach with the photos or other evidence such as the Housing Officer's statement to try and discern what the breach is. It is a practical problem that can lead to wasted time to trying to work out the exact breach alleged.

Displaying information

Regulation three of the Management Regulations is concerned with the displaying of information in the HMO and a Regulation often violated by managers and agents.

The Regulation states:

> *"3. The manager must ensure that—*
>
> *(a) his name, address and any telephone contact number are made available to each household in the HMO; and*
>
> *(b) such details are clearly displayed in a prominent position in the HMO."*

It is very easy to breach this Regulation and one that Housing Officers invariably prosecute (along with other breaches) landlords and agents for. The aim of this Regulation is public safety and for tenants to know who is the manager of the property and how to contact him in case of an emergency. Often, managers will complain that tenants will have their number stored on a phone and that they will know their details in any event. The regulation though is plain – the details must be stored in a prominent position in the HMO along with contact details being made available – the mere giving of a contact number will not do. One other recurrent complaint is that a tenant may have ripped down the details of the manager. This may afford a reasonable excuse defence. Questions then to be asked include how often the property was inspected and whether it was brought to the landlord's attention.

Fire Safety breaches

Regulation 4 breaches are the most common breaches focused by Local Authorities when prosecuting. As these matters concern fire safety it is common for several of the summonses to be in relation to these breaches.

The policy of the Local Authority in relation to HMO fire standards should be looked at. This is usually on their website on the specific HMO standards page. Reading Council, for instance, have very detailed fire safety policy for HMO's. Sadly, there is no co-ordination here and whereas some Local Authorities will have their own carefully drafted policy concerning minimum standards other Local Authorities will defer to LACORS – the national fire safety standards. LACORS is followed by London councils and is an extensive list of standards with a large part of it dedicated to appropriate systems in HMO's including for instance fire door and alarm system standards.

What I do now is go through each part of Regulation 4 and then the relevant LACORS standard where appropriate and how this links in with the Regulation. Plainly, some Councils will not follow the LACORS standards but where they do it is imperative to cross-reference LACORS (and the case studies on HMO's in LACORS) to the breach the LA say has occurred.

Regulation 4(1)(a) states:

> *(1) "Duty of manager to take safety measures*
>
> *4.—(1) The manager must ensure that all* ***means of escape*** *from fire in the HMO are—*
>
> *(a) kept free from obstruction; and*
>
> *(b) maintained in good order and repair"*

You will often face summonses that state the "means of escape" are not in good order or are obstructed. Typical examples include a lack of self-closers on fire doors or lockable doors from the inside of the property in which a key is required to the lock the door from the outdoors. Other examples include furniture blocking doors or exits. Self-closers are a particular concern to Housing officers and unscrewed closers will often be of concern during an HMO inspection.

Notices for means of escape

Under Regulation 4(3) the notice indicating the means of escape must be displayed in positions in the HMO to make them clearly visible to the occupiers. Regulation 4 (6) confirm this does not apply to any HMO with four tenants or fewer. Local HMO standards may also contain their own guidance as to the signage required in an HMO as does LACORS. Plainly, what is clearly visible depends on the type of HMO you have. What the regulation does make clear though (although guidance may differ) is that the notices are not mandatory but that if they are displayed must be clearly visible. Smaller shared HMO's will not require such notices or signs but if they are displayed (i.e the landlord decides to do more than the legal minimum) they must be displayed in a position that will be seen by occupiers. It is sometimes the case that the landlords will go above and beyond the relevant fire safety standards required by either LACORS or the local standards. This may for instance mean that a shared house with three or four students has beyond an interlinked heat detection system a grade A system more suitable for multi-story blocks. This does not mean that the same standards do not apply. What is critical is that the standards as mandated by LACORS or the relevant LA guidance are complied with. This should include inspections and maintenance as is appropriate of any fire safety equipment. LACORS has case studies of the types of fire systems required for properties which it is recommended all landlords and agents look at.

Protection from injury

Regulation 4(4) is a very general HMO duty. The relevant regulation is worth setting out in its entirety:

> *"(4) The manager must take all such measures as are reasonably required to protect the occupiers of the HMO from injury, having regard to—*
>
> *(a) the design of the HMO;*
>
> *(b) the structural conditions in the HMO; and*
>
> *(c) the number of occupiers in the HMO.*
>
> *(5) In performing the duty imposed by paragraph (4) the manager must in particular—*

(a) in relation to any roof or balcony that is unsafe, either ensure that it is made safe or take all reasonable measures to prevent access to it for so long as it remains unsafe; and

(b) in relation to any window the sill of which is at or near floor level, ensure that bars or other such safeguards as may be necessary are provided to protect the occupiers against the danger of accidents which may be caused in connection with such windows."

Regulation 4(4)(a)-(c) is open-ended. It is important to note, once more, that the regulation is not a counsel of perfection. Only "reasonable" measures need be taken. These can again be cross-referenced with the relevant Local Authority's HMO policies. Common violations include gaps in the floor which can be tripping hazard, floorboards that are not even and steps too high. Other more serious violations include gaps on holes in piping between floors which can lead to fire risks should a fire break out. Others include landlords who create extra inner rooms in properties. This invariably causes a fire risk as the room may not lead into a safe exit from the property but rather into a risk room such as a kitchen before leading into a safe exiting area. One will also see allegations in relation to lockable doors charged under this section. Hence, a property with non-latch lockable gates leading to the front of the property might be charged under this section. Non FD30 or FD60 fire doors may also be charged under this section.

One point of note is that under Regulation 4(4)(c) one must bear in mind the number of people in the property. Plainly, if no one is residing the property the measures may be less onerous than if there are several residents inside the property. This is important for student properties as they are often empty during the summer months whilst the students are back at home. Housing Officers may well go in during the summer months when works are being undertaken (or the property is not in the condition it would be when term starts) and no one is around. In that case the measures reasonably required will be less onerous than when the property is full of students even if the tenancy agreements have been signed as no-one may be resident in the property.

Unsafe balconies and roofs

Regulation 4(5)(a) is focused specifically on unsafe balconies and roofs. If a balcony or roof is unsafe you must make take all reasonable measure to make it safe or take all reasonable means to prevent access to the roof or balcony. Of course, each case will be different but merely telling residents, whether or not high-risk tenants, of the risks that a balcony or roof is unsafe may not suffice. If tenants are told not to go on the roof or balcony (until repaired) then a note should be taken and recorded. The access point should also be blocked if appropriate and reasonable.

Bars and safeguards for windows

Regulation 4(5)(b) concerns the provision of bars or other safeguards for windows near or at floor level. Such bars will be most relevant with windows looking out onto streets. The risk that someone will kick the window or that a stone may break it for instance might be minimal, but the regulation is plain that precautions need to be taken "as may be necessary".

Maintenance of water and drainage systems

Regulation 5 concerns the maintenance of water and drainage systems. The regulation provides:

> *"5.—(1) The manager must ensure that the water supply and drainage system serving the HMO is maintained in good, clean and working condition and in particular he must ensure that—*
>
> *(a)any tank, cistern or similar receptacle used for the storage of water for drinking or other domestic purposes is kept in a good, clean and working condition, with a cover kept over it to keep the water in a clean and proper condition; and*
>
> *(b)any water fitting which is liable to damage by frost is protected from frost damage.*
>
> *(2) The manager must not unreasonably cause or permit the water or drainage supply that is used by any occupier at the HMO to be interrupted.*
>
> *(3) In this regulation "water fitting" means a pipe, tap, cock, valve, ferrule, meter, cistern, bath, water closet or soil pan used in connection with the supply or use of water, but the reference in this definition to a pipe does not include an overflow pipe or the mains supply pipe."*

The key points are that any tank or cistern used for the domestic water storage (or drinking water) must be kept in a clean and good condition and with a cover on top of it to keep the water clean. Water fittings that might be damaged by frost (i.e. external to the property) must be protected from such frost in regulation 5(1)(b). Regulation 5(2) provides that water and drainage supply must not be unreasonably interrupted. This means that landlords in charge of water supply or the paying of bills for water have a duty to ensure that the water supply remains functioning without interruption save for a very good reason. One allegation that Housing Officers do make is that the drains or guttering are blocked with vegetation or debris and this the drainage system is not in a good, clean and working order. Note that the duty is not simply that the system needs to be in good order but also clean as well. A reasonable excuse here probably is not simply that the drainage was to be repaired or cleaned at a later unspecified date or that tenants had not pointed out the blockages or issues with the drainage during any inspections.

Gas and electrical checks

As will be familiar with all landlords, whether or not renting an HMO or a property to a family unit, the Regulations make provision for gas and electrical checks. Under regulation 6(1) the owner (save for a reasonable excuse) must supply to the LA the latest gas appliance testing certificate from a recognized engineer for any gas appliance with seven days of receiving the request in writing from the LA. The regulations make no deeming provisions as to when the request is said to be "received" by the owner. Is it when the request is deemed served in the ordinary course of the post or if any email is served before the close of the working day with seven days commencing from the next day? In addition, under regulation 6(2) all electrical equipment must be tested once every five years at the very latest by a qualified engineer with any test certificate sent to the LA again within seven days of a request. Like water with the gas and electrical supply must not be unreasonably interrupted to any occupier in the property. The statutory reasonable excuse defence applies.

Keeping the property in good repair

Regulation 7 mandates a wide ranging duty to maintain the property in good repair and summons arising from this regulation are common. It should be read in conjunction with regulation 11(2) which holds that:

> *"Any duty imposed by these Regulations to maintain or keep in repair are to be construed as requiring a standard of maintenance or repair that is reasonable in all the circumstances, taking account of the age, character and prospective life of the house and the locality in which it is situated."*

Under regulation 7(1) there are general duties in relation to the common parts of an HMO. The subsection provides:

> *"7.—(1) The manager must ensure that all common parts of the HMO are—*
>
> *(a) maintained in good and clean decorative repair;*
>
> *(b) maintained in a safe and working condition; and*
>
> *(c) kept reasonably clear from obstruction."*

Obstructions

Even if the HMO common parts, such as corridors, are clean they must be reasonably clear from obstructions which for some Housing Officers includes items such as furniture due to be taking away. The "good and clean" decorative repair means that plastering and wallpaper must be in a good condition. Housing Officers are liable to look for cracks in walls and then state that the property is not in good repair even if an old property (See Regulation 11(2) above).

There are specified duties relating to public safety that must be adhered to in Regulation 7(2) which provides:

> *"In performing the duty imposed by paragraph (1), the manager must in particular ensure that—*
>
> *(a) all handrails and banisters are at all times kept in good repair;*
>
> *(b) such additional handrails or banisters as are necessary for the safety of the occupiers of the HMO are provided;*
>
> *(c) any stair coverings are safely fixed and kept in good repair;*
>
> *(d) all windows and other means of ventilation within the common parts are kept in good repair;*
>
> *(e) the common parts are fitted with adequate light fittings that are available for use at all times by every occupier of the HMO; and*
>
> *(f) subject to paragraph (3), fixtures, fittings or appliances used in common by two or more households within the HMO are maintained in good and safe repair and in clean working order."*

Handrails and trips

Handrails that are provided must be kept in good repair "at all times" if provided. Any handrails must be well maintained and there is little leeway in relation to poorly maintained rails. In addition, regulation 7(2)(c) – the duty to ensure the good repair of carpets – is a common concern of Housing Officers. Frayed carpeting or covering that is loose can cause a tripping hazard. Carpeting must be "safely fixed" and in addition be "in good repair".

Lights and cleanliness

Commons parts must be supplied with lights fittings available "at all times". This means that broken or blown light bulbs in particular might lead a manager liable to committing an offence under regulation 7(2)(e) or 7(2)(f). One of the other issues to be aware of is the wide ranging liability imposed by regulation 7(2)(f). Dirty ovens and other similar kitchen appliances must not only be safe and in good repair but *clean* as well since this adjective qualifies the word "working". Hence, shared properties with dirty ovens or other communal appliances in a poor state (which might well be due to the occupiers) can render occupiers liable to offences. The caveat to regulation 7(2)(f) is that such an onerous duty "does not apply in relation to fixtures, fittings or appliances that the occupier is entitled to remove from the HMO or which are otherwise outside the control of the manager". Hence appliances that come with the property when rented would be covered by the section whereas those the owner has brought in himself would not be.

Gardens and fencing

The duties within regulation 7 extend to gardens. Under regulation 7(4)(a) communal yards, forecourts and outhouses must be kept in good repair. The most frequently used subsection deployed by Housing Officers is regulation 7(4)(b) which states that "gardens belonging to the HMO must be kept in a *safe and tidy condition*". It matters not that the garden is merely safe. It must also be tidy as well. Tenancy agreements may well have a section delegating responsibility for keeping the garden tidy to tenants but with inspections in which HMO owners can view the state of the garden themselves such a clause may not be sufficient to afford a reasonable excuse defence.

Section 7(4)(c) relates to adequate external fencing and walls. The section provides:

> *"(c) boundary walls, fences and railings (including any basement area railings), in so far as they belong to the HMO, are kept and maintained in good and safe repair so as not to constitute a danger to occupiers."*

Does the fence belong to the HMO?

One issue here of note is that the fence or wall must belong to the HMO – a matter for the prosecuting authority to prove. Although the words "in so far as they belong to the HMO" are used in the section, it is difficult to import on fences or walls that belong to neighbouring properties liability under the Management Regulations and this is well worth pursuing as a point before employing any reasonable excuse defence (if not obvious as to who the wall or fence belongs to). In addition, the duty is not that the fence or walls are merely kept in good and safe repair but that they are not further a danger to occupiers.

Under regulation 7(5) any part of the HMO not in use must be kept reasonably clean and free from refuse and litter. Although not a breach commonly seen it does mean that attics and rooms not in use must be kept in good order.

Breaching the good repair obligations

As can be seen regulation 7 is very easy to be in breach of. It has general obligations and specific obligations all of which are framed in wide terms. On a practical level the excuse of blaming the occupier for decorative issues and keeping the property in good repair may be of limited use. In relation to the general repairing obligations of landlords, a landlord is not liable for disrepair in demised premises unless and until the occupier draws the disrepair to his attention: *see British Telecommunications plc v Sun Life Assurance Society plc* [1996] Ch 69, at 78-9. This is of course not a criminal case or linked to HMO law but it is worth asking in the context of such defences how often the landlord inspected the property? Was he made aware of faults by the tenants? Was an inventory or checklist kept? How soon after the last check did the issue occur? In addition, will this be verified by tenants if they have given statements to the LA and are to be called as prosecution witnesses? Managing agents and landlords will often complain (if not invariably) that they did not know of the fault alleged. Such defences warrant careful scrutiny.

Clean units of accommodation

Under Regulation 8 the HMO manager is under a duty to ensure each unit of living accommodation is in a clean condition when initially supplied to the occupier save for when the furnishing and fixtures belong to the occupier. The relevant provision states:

> "**8.**—(1) Subject to paragraph (4), the manager must ensure that each unit of living accommodation within the HMO and any furniture supplied with it are in clean condition ***at the beginning of a person's occupation of it.***"

Hence, there is a potential criminal sanction for supplying an unclean room at the beginning of an occupier's tenancy. Appliances, fixtures and fitttings must be kept in good working order which do not belong to the manager. There exist further duties under regulation 8(2) – that fittings and appliances are kept in good clean working order ; that the internal structure of the living accommodation is kept in gooo repair ; that windows and ventilation must be kept in good repair. The caveat to regulation 8(2) is in regulation 8(3) which importantly states:

> *"(3) The duties imposed under paragraph (2) do not require the manager to carry out any repair the need for which arises in consequence of use by the occupier of his living accommodation otherwise than in a tenant-like manner."*

Regulation 8(5) defines a non-tenant like manner as:

> *"(5) For the purpose of this regulation a person shall be regarded as using his living accommodation otherwise than in a tenant-like manner where he fails to treat the property in accordance with the covenants or conditions contained in his lease or licence*

> *or otherwise fails to conduct himself as a reasonable tenant or licensee would do."*

This is the only reference in the Management Regulations to the lack of care by tenants (or their breach of licence or tenancy conditions).

CHAPTER SIX
CONVERTED SECTION 257 HMO MANAGEMENT REGULATIONS

It is important to note that converted blocks of flats which come under section 257 of the Housing Act 2004 have their own management regulation regime under the Licensing and Management of Houses in Multiple Occupation (Additional Provisions) (England) Regulations 2007. This regime which is similar to the section 254 non-converted blocks of flat regime does have some differences which it is important to bear in mind. The regime is again about public safety and ensuring that section 257 converted blocks of flats adhere to minimum standards but with some differences since some flats in the blocks may be owner occupied and the individual flats themselves may not be let to groups of tenants.

Regulation 3 – control over certain areas

Regulation 3(1)(a) makes it plain that the duties of managers of these HMOs only apply to such parts of the HMO over which it would be reasonable to expect the license holder in all the circumstances to exercise control. Regulation 3(1)(b) again gives managers of such properties some leeway as the standard of repair is what is reasonable in all circumstances taking into account the age, character and prospective life of the house along with the locality in which it is located. The point here is that some allowance can be made for the type of property being utilized but this clearly cannot be seen as *carte blanche* to allow old properties to go to rack and ruin.

Regulation 4 – duty to provide information

Regulation 4 mandates the duty of the manager to provide his name, address and phone contact number clearly displayed in a prominent position in the common parts of the HMO so that all occupiers can see it. This is a duty often neglected – it must be displayed in the common area and, as said, be in an obvious position seen by all tenants.

Safety measures

Regulation 5 – the duty to take safety measures – is framed in much the same way as the that for non-section 257 HMOs. Fire equipment must be in good order and the property in such a state as to protect occupiers from the risk of injury. The location of means of escape notices must be displayed in the common parts of the HMO so that they are clearly visible to all occupiers. The regulations contain similar duties to maintain the water and drainage supply, and supply on demand gas and electrical certificates within seven days. Regulation 8 is another wide ranging duty to ensure the common parts of the HMO are kept in good and safe repair and reasonably clear from obstruction. There is the same duty as in the section 254 HMOs to keep gardens safe and tidy and outbuildings, yards and forecourts used by more than two households within the section 257 HMO in good order and a clean condition.

The definition of common parts is the entrance door to the HMO and the entrance doors leading to each unit of accommodation within the HMO. It also includes all parts of the HMO as comprise staircases, lifts, passageways, corridors, halls, lobbies, entrances, balconies, porches and steps used by the occupiers of the units living accommodation to within the HMO to gain access to the entrance doors of their unit.

CHAPTER SEVEN
FIRE RISK ASSESSMENTS FOR HMOs

Alongside the Management Regulations a fire risk assessment must be undertaken on the common parts of an HMO under the Regulatory Reform (Fire Safety) Order 2005.

Responsible Person

In brief, this must be done by the "responsible person". If the organization employs more than five people than such a risk assessment must be written down. The Government Guidance on undertaking assessments on sleeping accommodation states:

> *"If you are the responsible person you must carry out a fire risk assessment which must focus on the safety in case of fire of all 'relevant persons'. It should pay particular attention to those at special risk, such as disabled people, those who you know have special needs and children, and must include consideration of any dangerous substance liable to be on the premises. Your fire risk assessment will help you identify risks that can be removed or reduced and to decide the nature and extent of the general fire precautions you need to take. If your organisation employs five or more people, your premises are licensed or an alterations notice is in force, you must record the significant findings of the assessment. It is good practice to record your significant findings in any case."*

Reviewing HMO risk assessments

Such assessments need to be reviewed as appropriate and if there is a change undertaken again. The relevant parts of article 9 of the Regulatory Reform (Fire Safety) Order 2005 provides:

> "*9.— Risk assessment*
>
> *(1) The responsible person must make a suitable and sufficient assessment of the risks to which relevant persons are exposed for the purpose of identifying the general fire precautions he needs to take to comply with the requirements and prohibitions imposed on him by or under this Order.*
>
> *(2) Where a dangerous substance is or is liable to be present in or on the premises, the risk assessment must include consideration of the matters set out in Part 1 of Schedule 1.*
>
> *(3) Any such assessment must be reviewed by the responsible person regularly so as to keep it up to date and particularly if—*
>
> *(a) there is reason to suspect that it is no longer valid; or*
>
> *(b) there has been a significant change in the matters to which it relates including when the premises, special, technical and organisational measures, or organisation of the work undergo significant changes, extensions, or conversions,*
>
> *and where changes to an assessment are required as a result of any such review, the responsible person must make them.*
>
> *(4) The responsible person must not employ a young person unless he has, in relation to risks to young persons, made or*

reviewed an assessment in accordance with paragraphs (1) and (5).

(5) In making or reviewing the assessment, the responsible person who employs or is to employ a young person must take particular account of the matters set out in Part 2 of Schedule 1.

(6) As soon as practicable after the assessment is made or reviewed, the responsible person must record the information prescribed by paragraph (7) where—

(a) he employs five or more employees;

(b) a licence under an enactment is in force in relation to the premises; or

(c) an alterations notice requiring this is in force in relation to the premises.

(7) The prescribed information is—

(a) the significant findings of the assessment, including the measures which have been or will be taken by the responsible person pursuant to this Order; and

(b) any group of persons identified by the assessment as being especially at risk."

The responsible person is defined in article 3(b) as

"(i) the person who has control of the premises (as occupier or otherwise) in connection with the carrying on by him of a trade, business or other undertaking (for profit or not); or

> *(ii) the owner, where the person in control of the premises does not have control in connection with the carrying on by that person of a trade, business or other undertaking"*

Depending on the arrangements this person may be the landlord or managing agent.

<u>Does an HMO come with the ambit of the Order</u>

Under Article 2 of the Order domestic premises (which are not covered by the Order) are defined as "premises occupied as a private dwelling (including any garden, yard, garage, outhouse, or other appurtenance of such premises <u>which is not used in common by the occupants of more than one such dwelling).</u>"

In other words, single private dwellings are not covered. The LACORS guidance (para 35) defines these properties that do not come within the 2005 Order as HMOs in which although all tenants are unrelated they have exclusive possession of the property under one tenancy – i.e. a typical shared student house. It is important to look at the provisions and ascertain whether in the HMO you are responsible for comes under the ambit of the 2005 Order.

In short, a risk assessment should be undertaken and written down if you employ five or more people and are the responsible person of an HMO in relation to the common parts of the HMO. If there is a change to the set up or design of the HMO a new risk assessment (or a review of the old assessment) ought to be carried out.

CHAPTER EIGHT THE CIVIL PENALTY REGIME

One of the core points to be aware of is the new discretion for Local Authorities to issue civil penalty notices under the Housing and Planning Act 2016 schedule 9. There are a number of conditions that must be complied with before such penalties can be issued. These civil penalties are well worth suggesting in written representations to the Local Authority and are very often of benefit to both sides in HMO cases. More and more LA are now developing their own policies as to the level of penalty and when a penalty is appropriate.

General Considerations on Civil Penalties

Some Local Authorities are indeed already boasting of the amounts raised through these penalties imposed for cases that may have been prosecuted in the past. It is a shortsighted LA that will not consider the imposition of such penalties in appropriate cases. General reasons for accepting civil penalties include:

a) The fact that a civil penalty can be spent by HMO Enforcement Teams as opposed to a court imposed fine with the only costs retainable by the Local Authority.

b) The LA can set the initial penalty subject to representations from the subject. Reasons need to be given for the imposition of the penalty but these need only be brief reasons by the LA. This avoids the need to prepare detailed witness statements for a prosecution.

c) The penalty for each breach can be up to £30000. Of course, a global view needs to be taken but the lack of a license can, for instance, be fined separately from each management breach.

d) The LA need only allow 28 days for representations before the immediate imposition of the penalty which if not appealed becomes payable to the LA.

e) The criteria for issuing a civil penalty are framed in as flexible and pragmatic a manner so as to be applied to a range of cases.

Guidance

There is detailed guidance on the new Civil Penalties regime from the Department of Communities and Local Government Civil Penalties in its *the Housing and PlanningAct 2016 Guidance for Local Housing Authorities* paper.

Offences applicable to the penalties

Civil penalties can be used for offences including failing to comply with an improvement notice, contravention of an overcrowding notice, failure to comply with management regulations in relation to HMO's and the fact of simply failing to register a property as an HMO. The penalty regime came into force on 6th April 2017 for offences committed after this date with a maximum penalty of £30000 per offence.

Guidance to take into account

Paragraph 3.5 of Guidance sets out the key factors in to be borne in mind when deciding whether to issue a civil penalty. It is of great importance and should be at the forefront of any written submissions to the LA if a client is to be prosecuted or being investigated for HMO breaches. The paragraph provides:

> *"What factors should a local housing authority take into account when deciding on the level of civil penalty? Local housing authorities have the power to impose a civil penalty of up to £30,000. They should develop and document their own policy on determining the appropriate level of civil penalty in a particular case. Generally, we would expect the maximum amount to be reserved for the very worst offenders. The actual amount levied in any particular case should reflect the severity of the offence, as well as taking account of the landlord's previous record of offending. Local housing authorities should consider the following factors to help ensure that the civil penalty is set at an appropriate level:*
>
> *a) Severity of the offence. The more serious the offence, the higher the penalty should be.*
>
> *b) Culpability and track record of the offender. A higher penalty will be appropriate where the offender has a history of failing to comply with their obligations and/or their actions were deliberate and/or they knew, or ought to have known, that they were in breach of their legal responsibilities. Landlords are running a business and should be expected to be aware of their legal obligations.*

c) The harm caused to the tenant. This is a very important factor when determining the level of penalty. The greater the harm or the potential for harm (this may be as perceived by the tenant), the higher the amount should be when imposing a civil penalty.

d) Punishment of the offender. A civil penalty should not be regarded as an easy or lesser option compared to prosecution. While the penalty should be proportionate and reflect both the severity of the offence and whether there is a pattern of previous offending, it is important that it is set at a high enough level to help ensure that it has a real economic impact on the offender and demonstrates the consequences of not complying with their responsibilities.

e) Deter the offender from repeating the offence. The ultimate goal is to prevent any further offending and help ensure that the landlord fully complies with all of their legal responsibilities in future. The level of the penalty should therefore be set at a high enough level such that it is likely to deter the offender from repeating the offence.

f) Deter others from committing similar offences. While the fact that someone has received a civil penalty will not be in the public domain, it is possible that other landlords in the local area will become aware through informal channels when someone has received a civil penalty. An important part of deterrence is the realisation that (a) the local housing authority is proactive in levying civil penalties where the need to do so exists and (b) that the level of civil penalty will be set at a high enough level to both punish the offender and deter repeat offending.

g) Remove any financial benefit the offender may have obtained as a result of committing the offence. The guiding principle here should be to ensure that the offender does not benefit as a result of committing an offence, i.e. it should not be cheaper to offend than to ensure a property is well maintained and properly managed."

Key factors

One of the core points here is that LA's are encouraged to issue penalties to ensure that there is no financial benefit to the landlord or agent for breaching HMO rules. One point of use is to consider providing the LA, based on this point, with the breakdown of the profit made during the period of offending in relation to the HMO so that the LA can calculate any penalty with one eye on those figures. A further "very important factor" is any harm caused to tenants. A penalty is more likely in cases in which no harm has been caused to tenants and where the culpability is due to ignorance as opposed to malice.

Track record of offender

The LA must also look at the track record of the offender and their level of compliance in the past. One other point is that the £30000 limit is the ceiling and should be for the worst offenders. It is worth standing back and asking whether the penalty issued (as I have seen with some clients) is proportionate to the offence. There are no set guidelines with these offences but penalties above £20000 should be reserved for particularly unpleasant fire safety or overcrowding offences and not offences involving lack of decorative repair or where someone who is not a property professional has not applied for a license especially in an area where there is selective licensing.

A Local Authority cannot prosecute and also at the same time instigate a civil penalty. A civil penalty cannot be issued if the matter is proceeding through the Courts. The only real option here is for the LA to discontinue criminal proceedings and to issue a civil penalty – the law is such that the LA cannot simply adjourn the criminal case pending the issuance (and payment) of a civil penalty. If a person is convicted then a civil penalty cannot, in addition, be imposed.

A civil penalty can be imposed for each separate breach of management regulations. The guidance specifically states that a civil penalty can be imposed on both the landlord and letting agent for failing to obtain a license for a licensable property. There is no difficulty in professional letting agents being prosecuted and landlords, relying on the advice of such agents, being given penalties depending on the circumstances of the case as an alternative. The penalty for each can differ.

Threshold for instigating civil penalties

The guidance mandates that before taking action and imposing a civil penalty the LA must be satisfied that if prosecuted in the magistrates' court there would be a realistic prospect of conviction bearing in mind the CPS Code for Crown Prosecutors as to whether sufficient evidence exists that would make the prospect of a conviction realistic. If the civil penalty is challenged in the First Tier Tribunal the LA would need to prove beyond reasonable doubt – to the criminal standard - that the offence has been committed. The relevant provision under the Housing Act s 249A states:

> *"(1) The local housing authority may impose a financial penalty on a person if satisfied, beyond reasonable doubt, that the person's conduct amounts to a relevant housing offence in respect of premises in England."*

Local Authorities are encouraged to develop their own policies and decide on a case by case basis based on those policies whether or not to instigate civil penalties. Even for serious offences, bearing in mind how high the penalty per breach can be, the guidance is firm in declaring that the mere fact an offence is serious should not mean that it should be prosecuted:

> *"Prosecution may be the most appropriate option where an offence is particularly serious or where the offender has committed similar offences in the past.* ***However, that does not mean civil penalties should not be used in cases where serious offences have been committed.*** *A civil penalty of up to £30,000 can be imposed where a serious offence has been committed and a local housing authority may decide that a significant financial penalty (or penalties if there have been several breaches), rather than prosecution, is the most appropriate and effective sanction in a particular case."*

LA's are advised to use existing powers to assess the landlords assets and income before determining the appropriate penalty. LA's should be sent to assist them accounts for the offender in appropriate cases so as to allow them to gauge the right penalty level. This can be done after the initial civil penalty notice and before the final notice is received.

Procedure for issuing a penalty

The procedure for issuing a civil penalty notice is relatively straightforward. The LA must give the offender a Notice of Intent which sets out the amount of the proposed penalty, the reasons for imposing the penalty and information about the right of the landlord to make representations

Importantly, the deadline for giving the notice is no later than six months after the LA has sufficient evidence of the conduct to which the penalty relates or at any time if the conduct is continuing – i.e satisfied so that it is sure that there is conduct amounting to an offence such that the LA can issue a notice of intent. A notice cannot be given more than six months beginning with the last day on which the conduct occurred. To give one example, if a landlord is being prosecuted for a management regulation breach in an HMO which does not need licensing and one tenant of three unrelated tenants vacates permanently leaving two there unrelated, it is no longer an HMO in law. The Management Regulations no longer bite and the day on which the tenant moved out would become the day from which limitation runs.

The LA can at any time in writing withdraw a notice of intent or final notice. It can also at any time reduce the amount specified in the notice of intent or final notice. This must include after the final notice has been issued if the matter is being appealed to the Property Tribunal. Hence, there is some scope to attempt a dialogue with the LA after issuing the appeal in relation to the final amount in particular.

CHAPTER NINE
SENTENCING IN THE COURTS

There are no set formal sentencing guidelines for sentencing those who breach HMO regulations. Fines from a few hundred pounds to tens of thousands of pounds have been issued by Courts at first instance.

An important case for practitioners is *Sumal & Sons (Properties) Ltd v Newham London Borough Council* [2012] EWCA Crim 1840. In this case the Court of Appeal held that a landlord convicted of an offence of having an unlicensed property in a selective licensing area who had had his rents whilst the property was unlicensed confiscated under the Proceeds of Crime Act 2002 had wrongly had these rents confiscated and that the Crown Court Judge had erred in agreeing that the rents were the proceeds of crime. The landlord had not obtained the rent "as a result of or in connection with" his criminal conduct, within the meaning of section 76(4) of the 2002 Act. What persuaded the Court that POCA did not apply as a way of extracting the rents whilst the property was unlicenced was the fact that the Housing Act 2004 makes clear provision for rent repayment orders whereby tenants can be paid back their rent whilst the property is unlicenced. One point the Court made, at paragraph 41 was:

> *"A yet further difficulty in the council's argument is this. If it were right, then that could mean that an errant landlord could both be liable (aside from any fine) to a rent repayment order under the 2004 Act and also be liable to a confiscation order in respect of the same offending. That would be double jeopardy or double recovery. Mr Paul acknowledged that would be so. But his answer was that "in practice" that would hardly ever*

happen (and had not happened here). In any case, a local housing authority would "choose one or the other" remedy, he asserted: or, if it elected to pursue both, the courts could then stay the confiscation proceedings as oppressive. That is not a sufficient answer. The very possibility of such a scenario is in itself an indication that Parliament had not intended the confiscation procedure to be available at all."

Although the case concerns a landlord having an unlicensed property in a selective licensing area this case plainly applies to breaches of licences in additional license areas of large HMOs which are simply not licenced at all. There is the simple, clear and well thought out remedy of rent repayment orders set down in the Housing Act 2004 which is the proper way to obtain the monies expended in rent when the property was rented in breach of the licensing requirements.

The Court also emphasized that fines should bring with them a "sting" (the paltry fine by the Recorder in this case was £2000) and that informally reported decisions were not very helpful:

"26 *Then Mr Rule sought to renew his grounds of challenge to the sentence. He submitted that the fine was excessive. He pointed to the defendant company's good record, to the fact that it would have got a licence had it applied for one and to the personal distractions of its managing director. He also pointed to the fact that the initial fee, on the introductory terms offered by the council, as discounted for a five-year licence would be £300 if promptly paid, rather than the indicated £500. Failure to apply for a licence has meant, under the publicised procedure, that the defendant would have to pay the full £500 licence fee and moreover that would only be for an initial one-year period.*

So, he submitted, that was quite a significant financial penalty suffered already by virtue of the failure to obtain the licence.

27 The fact remains that the defendant—an experienced, professional landlord—had, in the face of repeated warnings, chosen not to comply with its obligations. Further, there could be no mitigation for a plea as there had been a trial. The company has a substantial turnover of over £600,000 p a. It is in fact generally not particularly helpful to refer—as happened here in the Crown Court—to ***other informally reported decisions, to the extent that any can be found, as to the level of fines imposed in this particular Housing Act context—just because the amount of the fine will depend on the particular circumstances of the particular case and also will necessarily be geared to some extent to the ability of the landlord in question to pay a particular amount. Ordinarily, a fine in this context can also properly convey a degree of "sting" geared to a particular landlord's financial situation.*** *It is to be borne in mind that the maximum fine available in respect of a particular offence under section 95(1) for one particular house is £20,000. It could, in fact, be said that this fine in this particular case was, given the circumstances, on the moderate side—it may well be in part because, as the recorder had indicated, she was bearing in mind the amount of the confiscation order. At all events, Mr Rule's suggestion that the amount of the fine was excessive is unsustainable. His initial suggestion that in this case there should, as a matter of principle, have been a conditional discharge was completely unrealistic."*

Key principles

What is key is that:

a) **Fines should have a sting in the tail. The measly fine of £2000 in this case was criticized albeit with the caveat that confiscation may have been the reason why it was so low;**

b) **The fines should be based on the means of the landlord.** Accounts for three years if available should be brought to sentencing hearings;

c) POCA is not available although it is important to take into account **the profit made by the landlord or agent during the period in question when advising on the likely penalty;**

d) Matters are aggravated by the failure to heed warnings especially if the landlord is a professional landlord or letting agent.

One other very important factor to take into account is that informally reported decisions are not "particularly" helpful and should not be used as *Sumal* makes clear. The Court in this case did not expand on the term "informal" but this must apply to the media reports and sentencing reports on Local Authority news websites that are sometimes quoted at hearings to show the "range" of penalties in the local area for HMO offences. The obvious problems are that the underlying facts of such reports are not known. One doesn't know what the means of the offender are, what particular mitigation was put forward or, indeed, what credit was given for a guilty plea (if any).

CHAPTER TEN
FIT AND PROPER PERSONS FOR MANAGEMENT OF HMOs

Following a sentence, the other important matter to be aware of is that the LA's assess applicants for licences as to whether they are a fit and proper person to hold an HMO license (whether for large HMO's, selective licenses or additional licences). The business model of HMO landlords or agents can be put in jeopardy (or made far more difficult) if they are not held to be fit and proper persons. This is a point that ought not to be overlooked by advisers on the potential consequence of conviction since the revocation of licenses held at present or the refusal of future licenses is no small matter for an HMO owner or indeed the LA granting a shorter license than, say, a normal five year license.

Cases on fit and proper persons

In *London Borough of Waltham Forest v Reid* [2017] UKUT 396 (LC) the Upper Tribunal (Lands Chamber) held that matters relevant to whether a landlord was a fit and proper person in relation to the duration of a selective license was fact sensitive depending on the individual case. Fleshing this out somewhat the Tribunal did hold that relevant general matters might include where there is a continuing risk of housing law being breached or a "realistic risk" of a repeated breach. The Tribunal held that it was unreasonable for the LA policy to determine that a license was to be reduced to allow a relevant conviction to become spent (i.e one year for a fine to be deemed spent under the Rehabilitation of Offenders Act and hence, in this case, the license was reduced to one year from the normal five year period). The Tribunal took a more flexible approach – depending on the facts of any case a conviction may or may not be relevant.

Reid, on the facts, is of some note. In this case the appellant was fined £10000 for five breaches of failing to license five properties in selective licencing areas with new licenses granted for one year as opposed to the normal five years. Mr Reid had been a landlord since 1990 without complaint bar one in 2015 from a tenant which had been resolved. The findings of the First Tier Tribunal (with the appeal upheld by the Upper Tribunal) were that the convictions related to one single omission for failing to license five properties when the new license requirements in Waltham Forest came into place. There was no evidence of significant disrepair or failure to apply for other regulatory requirements. He had simply not been aware of the new selective licensing system until he had received a letter in November 2015. He had not received the letter in August 2015 in relation to the new requirements. After receiving the LA's letters in November he had applied for Temporary Exemption Notices in relation to the property with the application refused in December 2015. He had been issued summons for the offences in March 2016. The Upper Tribunal agreed that the licenses could be for five years as was normal rather than for one year. <u>What is also of note is that the mere fact of the conviction did not stop him obtaining a licence with the issue only as to the length of the licence.</u>

<u>Statutory test on fit and proper person</u>

The statutory test for whether a potential applicant for an HMO licence is a fit and proper person is contained in section 66 of the Housing Act 2004. The Local Housing Authority must have regard to whether the manager or license holder (or someone associated or formerly associated with them and is relevant to whether the applicant is a fit and proper person) has committed any fraud offences, dishonesty offences, offences involving drugs or violence or any sexual offence attracting notification requirements. The LA can also take into account whether the person has contravened any provision of the law relating to housing or landlord and tenant law or practiced unlawful discrimination in their business. A person is not a fit and proper person if a banning order under section 16 of the Housing and Planning Act 2016 is in order. The LA must also assess whether any manager has sufficient competence to manage an HMO. HMO applications will have boxes in them for HMO licences in which convictions and breaches of law will need to be declared.

In *Waltham Forest v Khan* [2017] UKUT 153 (LC) it was held in relation to selective licences that a landlord's compliance with planning requirements was relevant to the issue of licensing. The same principle must apply to HMO. Licencing and planning control "were not unconnected policy spheres".

It should be noted that the Section 21 procedure cannot be used to terminate a tenancy if the property is an unlicenced HMO.

Rogue Landlord's Database

In addition, convicted landlords and agents will appear on name and shame rogue landlord registers. In London the register can be found at https://www.london.gov.uk/rogue-landlord-checker. The name of the agent or landlord convicted, level of fine and offence committed all appear on the database. In addition, names and details stay on the data base for one year – the length it takes a fine to be spent under the Rehabilitation of Offenders Act 1974. This is a very powerful motive not to offend in itself.

CHAPTER ELEVEN
THE RENT REPAYMENT ORDERS REGIME

Aside from fines, convictions and the difficulties that can arise with further HMO licensing if not declared a fit and proper person landlords and agents may also find that Rent Repayment Orders are made against them. With the ease of applying for such orders and the potential amounts offenders could be on the line for it is worth considering these orders in more detail. Since April 2017 the relevant law has been sections 44 to 50 of the Housing and Planning Act 2016.

If a tenant is applying for a RRO for a landlord having an unlicenced HMO the maximum amount of rent that can be repaid back is 12 months. In particular, the Tribunal can take into account when calculating the amount to be paid back the conduct of the landlord and the tenant, the financial circumstances of the landlord along with whether the landlord has been convicted of the offences to which RRO are targeted at which includes:

a) Failure to comply with an Improvement Notice under section 30 of the Housing Act 2004,

b) Failure to comply with a Prohibition Order under section 32 of the Hosing Act 2004, B

c) Breach of a banning order made under section 21 of the Housing and Planning Act 2016,

d) Using violence to secure entry to a property under section 6 of the Criminal Law Act 1977,

e) *Illegal eviction or harassment of the occupiers of a property under section 1 of the Protection from Eviction Act 1977.*

f) *Failure to license an HMO contrary to section 72(1) of the Housing Act 2004*

g) *Failure to license contrary to section 95(1) of the Housing Act 2004*

An application by a tenant must be made within twelve months of the date of the offence. In addition, the Tribunal must be satisfied beyond reasonable doubt that an offence has occurred.

HMO licensing failure exemption

Under section 46 a conviction for failing to license a property as an HMO is not one of the offences for which the maximum twelve months rent must be made back save for exceptional circumstances that would make is unreasonable for that amount to be paid back if the tenant is applying. Such a penalty (with the very narrow caveat of exceptional circumstances) is to be issued for convictions for the other offences listed above at a-e that a landlord is convicted of or if the landlord has been given a civil penalty. Local Authorities if making the application can claim back the full benefits paid (up to 12 months) for unlicenced HMOs and unlicenced properties under section 95(1) as well as for the other matters listed at a to e above save if there exist exceptional circumstances.

Local Authorities are further empowered to assist tenants if they wish to claim back rent and can make the application themselves.

Deciding whether to apply for an RRO

In deciding whether to apply for a rent repayment order under the 2016 Department of Communities and Local Government Guidance Local Authorities must have regard to the following if a landlord has not been convicted of an offence (as there is then a discretion as to how much is to be paid back):

> *"a. Punishment of the offender. Rent repayment orders should have a real economic impact on the offender and demonstrate the consequences of not complying with their responsibilities. Factors that a local housing authority may wish to consider include the conduct of the landlord and tenant, the financial circumstances of the landlord and whether the landlord has previously been convicted of similar offences;*
>
> *b. Deter the offender from repeating the offence. The level of the penalty should be set at a high enough level such that it is likely to deter the offender from repeating the offence;*
>
> *c. Dissuade others from committing similar offences. Rent repayment orders are imposed by the First-tier Tribunal and so the fact someone has received a rent repayment order will be in the public domain. Robust and proportionate use of rent repayment orders is likely to help ensure others comply with their responsibilities.*
>
> *d. Remove any financial benefit the offender may have obtained as a result of committing the offence. This is an important element of rent repayment orders: the landlord is forced to repay rent, and thereby loses much, if not all, of the benefit that accrued to them by not complying with their responsibilities."*

Cases on Rent Repayment Orders

In AB v The London Borough of Newham [2017] UKUT 299 (LC) the Upper Tribunal set aside a rent repayment order. The First Tier Tribunal had failed to take into account the mental health of the appellant in sufficient detail in its reasons although this was partially due to the appellant, in person, not wanting – as she erroneously thought would happen – her medical documents to be publicised or attending the hearing. The decision was also wrong as the appellant had been acquitted at the Crown Court of having an unlicenced HMO on appeal. The First Tier Tribunal had taken into account the wrong statutory test in deciding that there was a presumption that full payment had to be made of the 12 months Housing Benefit rent received rent save for exceptional circumstances when in fact the test was far looser due to the fact that the appellant had been acquitted. The Tribunal had to look the financial circumstances and conduct of the appellant and moreover choose a sum "reasonable in the circumstances". What is of interest is that she had sent detailed representations as to what appears to have been a serious mental health condition to Newham (having been acquitted of the offence in the Crown Court) which nevertheless went ahead and proceeded with the application for Rent Repayment Order.

In *Fallon v Wilson* [2014] UKUT 0300 (LC) the Upper Tribunal found a Residential Property Tribunal had erred in refunding the entirety of the rent paid to three tenants. One factor taken into account was that the landlord was not a professional landlord and only had one property he rented out. Two of the five tenants had not even applied for a RRO. There were no apparent complaints and there were only minor matters of disrepair. The period of not having a licence had been short before the landlord's conviction at the magistrates' court (a mere four months from the facts of the case before a licence was applied for).

Parker – core guidance on RRO

Parker v Waller ([2012] UKUT 301 (LC) was the first examination of Rent Repayment Orders by the Upper Tribunal in which the President of the Lands Tribunal laid down some guidance on such orders after an exploration of what their purpose was at paragraph 26. This included a concern the need for professional landlords to be dealt in a harsher manner than amateurs, the necessity of taking into account the fine at court and the deductions available for utility payments when a RRO is made:

> *"(i) Since the RRO provisions are in their nature penal, an RPT must be satisfied on every matter that is determinative of the tenant's entitlement to an order or its amount. It must be satisfied of the matters set out in section 73(8) , and it must take into account the particular matters set out in section 74(6) as well as any other matters that may be material.*
>
> ***(ii) Since the landlord is liable to suffer two penalties – a fine and an RRO – it will be necessary to take this into account. An RPT should have regard to the total amount that the landlord would have to pay by way of a fine and under an RRO. There may be a tension between the imposition of a fine and the making of an RRO. The maximum fine is £20,000, and this shows the seriousness with which Parliament regards the offence.** In the present case the magistrates imposed a fine of £525, which would suggest that they did not consider this particular offence to be other than minor. The*

RPT, however, is entitled to take a different view about the seriousness of operating the HMO without a licence.

(iii) ***There is no presumption that the RRO should be for the total amount received by the landlord during the relevant period unless there are good reasons why it should not be****. The RPT must take an overall view of the circumstances in determining what amount would be reasonable.*

(iv) Paragraph (a) of section 74(6) requires the RPT to take into account the total amount of rent received during any period during which it appears to it that the offence was being committed. It needs to do that because the RRO can only be made in respect of rent received during that period. It is limited to the period of 12 months ending with the date of the occupier's application (see section 74(8)). But the RPT ought also to have regard to the total length of time during which the offence was being committed, because this bears upon the seriousness of the offence.

(v) The fact that the tenant will have had the benefit of occupying the premises during the relevant period is not, in my judgment a material consideration or, if it is material, one to which any significant weight should be attached. This is because it is of the essence of an occupier's RRO that the rent should be repaid in respect of a period of his occupation. While the tenant might be viewed as the fortunate beneficiary of the sanction that is imposed on the landlord, it is only misconduct on his part (see paragraph(e)) that would in my view justify the reduction of a repayment amount that was otherwise reasonable.

(vi) ***Payments made as part of the rent for utility services count as part of the periodical payments in respect of which***

> ***an RRO may be made. But since the landlord will not himself have benefited from these, it would only be in the most serious case that they should be included in the RRO.***
>
> *(vii) Paragraph (d) requires the RPT to take account of the conduct and financial circumstances of the landlord. The circumstances in which the offence was committed are always likely to be material.* ***A deliberate flouting of the requirement to register will obviously merit a larger RRO than instances of inadvertence – although all HMO landlords ought to know the law. A landlord who is engaged professionally in letting is likely to be more harshly dealt with than the non-professional."***

In short, the tribunals will give little leeway to professional letting agents or landlords who fail to register properties as compared to inadvertent errors with consideration to be paid to the fines landlords can face at court.

CHAPTER TWELVE
CONCLUSION

There can be little excuse for landlords and agents to fall foul of the regulatory regime in relation to HMOs. If one does, the law gives Local Authorities a wide range of powers with the issue very often one of mitigation as opposed to defence. It is critical to ensure compliance with all conditions and all licencing requirements as prevention is far better in the HMO world then expensive and difficult cures. On a practical level properties should be inspected regularly. Fire safety should be at the forefront of the HMO owner's mind and any concerns from experienced Housing Officers should be allayed as soon as possible. Landlords and agents should be well aware of the consquences of a conviction.

The consequences as can be seen above of a breach of HMO law are rightly draconian from all perspectives as the Courts and Local Authorities prioritise public safety in HMO's alongside the need to deter landlords from committing these offences.

'A Practical Guide to Inheritance Act Claims by Adult Children Post-Ilott v Blue Cross' by Sheila Hamilton Macdonald

'A Practical Guide to Elderly Law' by Justin Patten

'Arguments and Tactics for Personal Injury and Clinical Negligence Claims' by Dorian Williams

'A Practical Guide to QOCS and Fundamental Dishonesty' by James Bentley

'A Practical Guide to Drone Law' by Rufus Ballaster, Andrew Firman, Eleanor Clot

'Practical Mediation: A Guide for Mediators, Advocates, Advisers, Lawyers, and Students in Civil, Commercial, Business, Property, Workplace, and Employment Cases' by Jonathan Dingle with John Sephton

'Practical Horse Law: A Guide for Owners and Riders' by Brenda Gilligan

'A Comparative Guide to Standard Form Construction and Engineering Contracts' by Jon Close

'A Practical Guide to Compliance for Personal Injury Firms Working With Claims Management Companies' by Paul Bennett

'A Practical Guide to the Landlord and Tenant Act 1954: Commercial Tenancies' by Richard Hayes & David Sawtell

'A Practical Guide to Personal Injury Claims Involving Animals' by Jonathan Hand

'A Practical Guide to Psychiatric Claims in Personal Injury' by Liam Ryan

'Introduction to the Law of Community Care in England and Wales' by Alan Robinson

'A Practical Guide to Dog Law for Owners and Others' by Andrea Pitt

'Ellis and Kevan on Credit Hire – 5th Edition' by Aidan Ellis & Tim Kevan

'RTA Allegations of Fraud in a Post-Jackson Era: The Handbook – 2nd Edition' by Andrew Mckie

'RTA Personal Injury Claims: A Practical Guide Post-Jackson' by Andrew Mckie

'On Experts: CPR35 for Lawyers and Experts' by David Boyle

'An Introduction to Personal Injury Law' by David Boyle

'A Practical Guide to Claims Arising From Accidents Abroad and Travel Claims' by Andrew Mckie & Ian Skeate

'A Practical Guide to Cosmetic Surgery Claims' by Dr Victoria Handley

Printed in Great Britain
by Amazon

57810950R00059